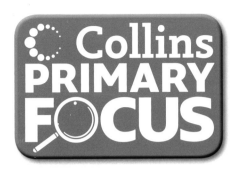

Vocabulary

Pupil Book 1

Louis Fidge and Sarah Lindsay

William Collins' dream of knowledge for all began with the publication of his first book in 1819. A self-educated mill worker, he not only enriched millions of lives, but also founded a flourishing publishing house. Today, staying true to this spirit, Collins books are packed with inspiration, innovation and practical expertise. They place you at the centre of a world of possibility and give you exactly what you need to explore it.

Collins. Freedom to teach.

Published by Collins
An imprint of HarperCollins*Publishers* Ltd.
77–85 Fulham Palace Road
Hammersmith
London
W6 8JB

**Browse the complete Collins catalogue at
www.collinseducation.com**

Text © Louis Fidge and Sarah Lindsay 2013
Design and illustrations © HarperCollins*Publishers* 2013

Previously published as *Collins Primary Writing*, first published 1998; and *Collins Focus on Writing*, first published 2002.

10 9 8 7 6 5 4 3 2 1

ISBN: 978-0-00-750100-7

British Library Cataloguing in Publication Data
A Catalogue record for this publication is available from the British Library.

Cover template: Laing & Carroll
Cover illustration: Paul McCaffrey
Series design: Neil Adams
Illustrations: Stephanie Dix and Emily Skinner.
Some illustrations have been reused from the previous edition (978-0-00-713226-3).

Printed and bound by Printing Express Limited, Hong Kong.

Contents

Dictionaries are arranged in **alphabetical order**.
Dictionaries give us the **definitions** (meanings) of words.
Dictionaries help us to **check spellings**.

This page comes near the end of my dictionary.

alphabetical order

definitions

Some words have more than one definition.

vanish	to disappear suddenly
vehicle	a machine such as a car, bus or lorry that carries people or goods from place to place
volume	1. one of a set of books 2. the amount of space filled by something 3. the loudness of a sound
vulture	a large bird that feeds on dead animals

checking spellings

vulcher

Have I spelled this word correctly?

Practice

Copy and complete these sentences.

1. Dictionaries help us check the s p e l l i n g of words.
2. Dictionaries are arranged in a _ _ _ _ _ _ _ _ _ _ _ _ o _ _ _ _.
3. Dictionaries give us the d _ _ _ _ _ _ _ _ _ _ of words.

More to think about

Use a dictionary to look up these words. Write a definition for each word.

1. These words are found at the beginning of the dictionary.

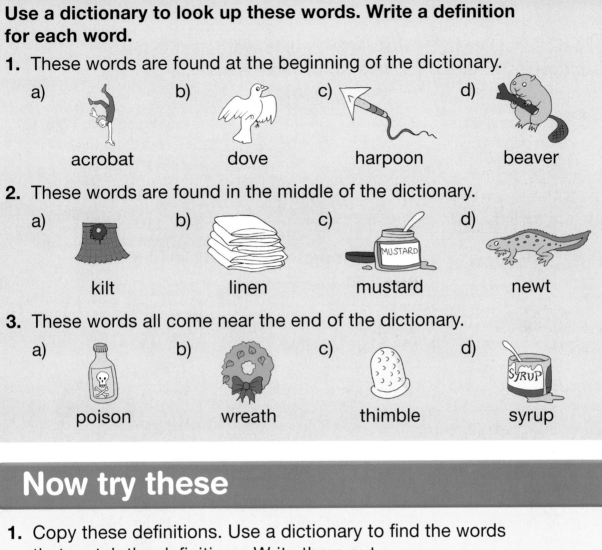

   a)   acrobat   b)   dove   c)   harpoon   d)   beaver

2. These words are found in the middle of the dictionary.

   a)   kilt   b)   linen   c)   mustard   d)   newt

3. These words all come near the end of the dictionary.

   a)   poison   b)   wreath   c)   thimble   d)   syrup

Now try these

1. Copy these definitions. Use a dictionary to find the words that match the definitions. Write them out.

   a) a bird that cannot fly: os <u>t</u> <u>r</u> <u>i</u> <u>c</u> <u>h</u>

   b) this makes things look bigger: micro _ _ _ _ _

   c) a large church: ab _ _ _ _

2. Use a dictionary to find a definition for each of these words. Write out the words and definitions.

   a) restaurant   b) panda   c) statue   d) burglar

3. Use a dictionary to check the spellings of these words. If the word is misspelled, write it out correctly.

   a) parashoot   b) pyramid   c) sholder   d) electrisity

In a dictionary there are usually two **guide words** at the top of each page. They help you find words more quickly and easily.

This tells you the first word on page 47.		This tells you the last word on page 47.

crush   *page* 47   **cuddle**

crush   to squash or press something so hard that it is broken

cry   1. to let tears fall from your eyes
2. to shout loudly

cube   a solid object with six equal square surfaces

cucumber   a long, green salad vegetable

cuddle   to put your arms closely around something or someone you love

Practice

Write answers to these questions.

1. Which is the first word on the dictionary page above?
2. Which is the last word on the dictionary page above?
3. With which letter do all the words on the dictionary page begin?
4. Would the page be near the beginning or the end of the dictionary?

More to think about

Copy and complete the sentences. Use a dictionary to help you.
When you've finished, write the words in alphabetical order.

1. A sh <u>a</u> <u>r</u> <u>k</u> is a large fish that sometimes attacks people.
2. A str <u>a w b e rr y</u> is a soft, red fruit.
3. A syc _ _ _ _ _ _ is a type of tree.
4. A sur g e on is a doctor who performs operations.

Now try these

1. Copy the lists and match the guide words to the word that should
   appear on the same page.

   spire to **spread**   well

   heat to **helpless**   lock

   weather to **whale**   splash

   living to **lollipop**   track

   towel to **travel**   purpose

   public to **pyramid**   hedgehog

2. Copy the questions and write a word that could fit between each of
   these guide words.

   a) shape ___<u>sleep</u>___ snooze   b) fly _____ friend

   c) bank _____ brush   d) pen _____ purse

Unit 3

Using a thesaurus

A **thesaurus** is a book that contains synonyms.
Synonyms are words that have **similar meanings**.

main word

type of word

synonyms

A thesaurus is arranged in **alphabetical order**.

tall	*adj.*	big, lofty, high
tank	*n.*	1. armoured vehicle, combat car
		2. reservoir, cistern, vat
teach	*v.*	inform, tell, instruct, educate, show, explain
terrible	*adj.*	horrible, vile, frightful, fearful, dreadful
thaw	*v.*	melt, dissolve, defrost
thief	*n.*	burglar, crook, robber, pilferer
thirsty	*adj.*	arid, dry, parched

adj. = adjective
n. = noun
v. = verb

Practice

1. Copy and complete these sentences.

   a) A thesaurus is a book that contains s y n o n y m s.

   b) Synonyms are words with similar m _ _ _ _ _ _ _.

2. Use the thesaurus page above to write the answers to these questions.

   a) What are the three synonyms for the word "tall"?

   b) Which three words mean the same as "melt"?

   c) Which word has two different meanings?

   d) Which of the main words are nouns?

More to think about

Copy the sentences. Replace each underlined word with a synonym.
Use the thesaurus page on page 6 to help you.

1. Mum tried to <u>teach</u> Jo how to tie a bow.
2. The icicles began to <u>thaw</u>.
3. The <u>thief</u> broke into the house.
4. The <u>tall</u> giant climbed down the beanstalk.
5. The <u>tank</u> lumbered noisily along.
6. Tom looked out of the window at the <u>terrible</u> weather.

Now try these

1. Write a sentence for each of these words.
   a) soak
   b) nudge
   c) blot out
   d) consume
   e) punch
   f) sparkle
   g) guard
   h) wonderful

2. Now use the thesaurus to find some synonyms for each word in Question 1.

Unit 4 Using context clues

When we don't know the meaning of a word, we can sometimes get **clues** from a picture or the words around it.

The smog was so thick it made it hard to see.
It made the children cough.

Practice

Use the picture clues to answer these questions.
Write down how you can tell the answer.

1. Has an aeroplane just been over?

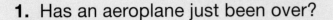

2. Was the window broken from the outside?

3. Has the bus just gone?

4. Has the weather been dry?

5. How many people had a meal?

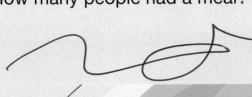

More to think about

Write the meaning of each underlined word. Check your answers in a dictionary. Use the pictures and sentences to help you.

1. The sun began to sink below the <u>horizon</u>.
2. The man was lying in a <u>hammock</u>.
3. The monk lived in a <u>monastery</u>.

Now try these

Work out and write the meaning of each underlined word. Use the sentences to help you. Check your answers using a dictionary.

1. The author sent the publishers a copy of his new book, but he kept a <u>duplicate</u> of it for himself.
2. The teacher knew something was wrong when she saw Lewis <u>gesticulating</u> wildly.
3. When you plant seeds, you must <u>saturate</u> them first.
4. The only form of <u>illumination</u> in the castle was oil lamps.
5. The police officer didn't believe the burglar's <u>account</u> of what happened.

Root words

A **prefix** is a group of letters added to the **beginning** of a root word.
A **suffix** is a group of letters added to the **end** of a root word.
They change the meaning of a **root word** in a particular way.

like   **dis**like

warm   warm**ly**

Practice

1. Match the correct root word to each picture. Write the words in the correct order.

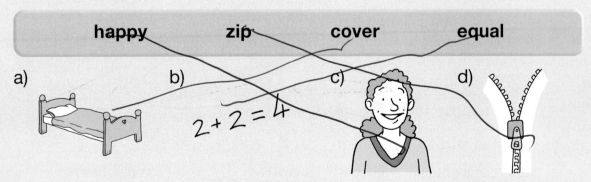

happy   zip   cover   equal

a)   b)   c)   d)

2+2=4

2. Now write the antonym (opposite meaning) of each word by adding the prefix **un**.

More to think about

Copy the story. Fill in each gap with a suitable word from the box. Circle the root word in each word.

return   unhappy   reunited   uncertain
disappeared   disobey   uneven

If you don't understand a word, look it up in your dictionary.

Ben looked un(happy)____. Lorna, his dog, had run away. Ben was _____ about what he should do. Should he _____ home or should he stay? Suddenly, he heard his mum call. He didn't want to _____ her but he didn't want to leave Lorna either.

"Where have you _____ to?" shouted his mum. "Lorna came home without you."

Ben couldn't believe his ears. He raced over the _____ playground and was soon happily _____ with Lorna.

Now try these

1. Match each root word with its correct suffix. Write out
   the new words.
   Remember, some words will match more than one suffix!

   | ly | ful | ness |

   hope
   wonder
   blind
   kind
   fresh
   smart
   dark
   vivid
   loud
   pain
   mouth
   ill
   quiet
   spite
   actual

2. Write four sentences.
   Use a word ending in **ly**, **ful** or **ness** in each sentence.
   Underline the words with these suffixes.

Dialogue words

Dialogue words describe how people **say** things.

Teacher said,

"You can use mumbled and muttered, groaned, grumbled and uttered, professed, droned or stuttered ... but don't use SAID!

"You can use rant or recite, yell, yodel or snort, bellow, murmur or moan, you can grunt or just groan ... but don't use SAID!"

... SAID my teacher.

Judith Nichols

Practice

Copy the sentences. Underline the dialogue words.

1. "What are you doing?" Mrs Shahidi <u>asked</u>.
2. "I am looking for my gerbil," replied Tom.
3. "Help! There's a large rat in my bag!" Samir shrieked.
4. "Don't worry. It's the gerbil!" exclaimed Anna.
5. "Perhaps it is looking for something to eat," Tara added.
6. "Put the gerbil back in the cage and get on with your work," Mrs Shahidi said.

More to think about

Copy the sentences. Choose the best dialogue word from the box to complete each sentence.

| replied   exclaimed   asked   added |

1. "Where does a baby ape sleep?" Kevin _____.
   "In an apricot!" his father _____ with a grin.

2. "What a lovely view!" _____ Kirsty.
   "You can see a long way," _____ Sam.

Now try these

1. Write a synonym for each of these words. Use a thesaurus to help you.

   a) whisper   b) call   c) say   d) shout
   e) exclaim   f) cry   g) ask   h) reply
   i) sigh   j) mutter

2. Choose a page from a book that has speech in it. Write down all the dialogue words you can find.

Antonyms

Antonyms are words that have opposite **meanings**.

A pet cat is **tame** but a lion is **wild**.

These words are **opposite** in **meaning**.

Practice

Copy the words. Underline the pair of antonyms in each set.

1. fat <u>easy</u> <u>difficult</u>
2. nasty thin nice
3. full bent straight
4. hot near cold
5. up top down
6. rude wet polite wrong
7. smooth ugly beautiful short
8. blue expensive soft cheap
9. fat heavy thin rough
10. awake tired happy asleep
11. rough gigantic smooth huge

More to think about

Copy these sentences. Fill in each gap with
a suitable antonym.

1. My hair is curly but Sam has <u>straight</u> hair.
2. Tom is noisy but Ahmed is _____.
3. Pat is polite but Ben is _____.
4. Mr Drew walks slowly but his wife walks _____.
5. I like to save my money but Shirin likes to _____ hers.
6. The blue bag is empty but the red bag is _____.

Now try these

Rewrite these sentences. Change each underlined word
to its antonym.

1. Our class is the <u>best</u> in the school.
2. My dog is very <u>obedient</u>.
3. Charlotte always comes to school <u>early</u>.
4. The rabbit <u>vanished</u> in a flash.
5. I looked for the <u>entrance</u>.
6. The judge said the man was <u>guilty</u>.

Unit 8 Synonyms

Synonyms are words with **similar meanings**.
You can use a **thesaurus** to find **synonyms** for words.

The giant was **huge**. His wife was also **enormous**.

These words are **synonyms**. They are **similar** in meaning.

Practice

1. Copy out the lists and match each word in Set A with its synonym in Set B. Copy out the matching words.

Set A	Set B
big	bad
break	smash
like	large
nice	enjoy
nasty	pleasant

   big – large

2. Copy these sentences. Replace the underlined word with a synonym. Use a thesaurus to help you.

   a) Emma lives in a <u>big</u> house.

   b) A vase will <u>break</u> if you drop it.

   c) I <u>like</u> playing games.

   d) It was a <u>nice</u> day.

   e) There was a <u>nasty</u> smell coming from the dustbin.

More to think about

1. Copy these sets of synonyms. Underline the odd word out.

   a) good   kind   friendly   burst   b) cold   huge   icy   frosty

   c) eat   happy   chew   gobble   d) fair   look   stare   peep

2. Copy the sentences. Choose one of the words from the box to fill each gap.

   | looked   stared   peeped |

   a) The lady _stared_ in amazement at the girl with pink hair.

   b) The boy _____ through the keyhole.

   c) I _____ at my shopping list to see what I needed.

Now try these

1. Use a thesaurus to help you find the missing synonyms. Write them out.

   a) speak   t <u>a</u> l k   b) hurry   r _ _ _ _

   c) observe   l _ _ _   d) beautiful   p _ _ _ _ _ _

   e) locate   f _ _ _   f) stroll   w _ _ _ _

2. Choose one synonym from each pair above.
   Make up a sentence for each word you choose.

3. Use a thesaurus to find three synonyms for each of these words.
   Write them out.

   a) go   b) happy   c) hot   d) nice   e) good   f) little

Homophones

Homophones are words that **sound the same** but have **different spellings and meanings**.

I love the fair!

I had to pay the fare to go on the ride.

Practice

Copy out the lists and match the homophone pairs by joining them with a line.

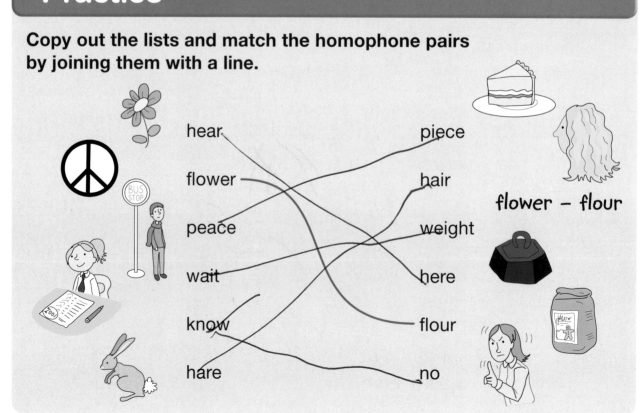

hear   piece

flower   hair

peace   weight

wait   here

know   flour

hare   no

flower – flour

More to think about

Copy each sentence and write the correct homophone in the gap.

1. "Can I ___pour___ the gravy on my food?" asked Tammy. (pour or paw)

2. Robert and Taylor asked which _____ they should go. (weigh or way)

3. The _____ flew through the thunderstorm. (plain or plane)

4. There were _____ puddings to choose from. (to or two)

5. "Don't _____ the paper!" exclaimed the teacher. (waste or waist)

6. Katie _____ her bike to school. (road or rode)

Now try these

1. Write a homophone for each of these words.

   a) brake
   b) blew
   c) whole
   d) to
   e) eight
   f) steel
   g) tail
   h) sum
   i) sea

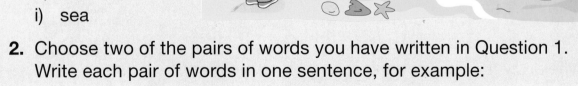

2. Choose two of the pairs of words you have written in Question 1. Write each pair of words in one sentence, for example:

   Tuhil wore his <u>blue</u> hat even though the wind <u>blew</u> it off a number of times.

Homonyms are words that have the **same spelling**, but **different meanings**.

I gave a **wave** as I splashed in the **wave**.

Practice

Copy these sentences. Underline the homonyms.

1. The pirate's treasure chest was full of gold.
   The pirate has a hairy chest.

2. My best pen is broken.
   You put sheep in a pen.

3. I spread jam on my bread.
   The car's stuck in a traffic jam.

4. There's no water in the tank.
   The army tank's very noisy.

5. Quick, bail out the boat, it's sinking!
   We're missing a bail on the cricket stumps.

More to think about

Copy these sentences. Complete them with the most suitable homonyms from the box.

> **match**　　**calf**　　**ring**　　**bow**

1. The girl had a _____bow_____ in her hair.
   The archer put an arrow in his _____.

2. On television there was a football _____.
   I struck a _____ to light the candle.

3. The lady wears a _____ on her finger.
   I heard the telephone _____ in the kitchen.

4. A baby cow is called a _____.
   The part of my leg between my knee and my ankle is my _____.

Now try these

Write pairs of sentences using the homonyms below. Remember the same homonym must have a different meaning in each sentence. Use a dictionary to help if you wish.

1. palm
2. tie
3. fly
4. toast
5. skirt
6. patient
7. tear
8. quiver
9. lift

Compound words

A **compound word** is made from two small words joined together.

playground
play + ground

Practice

Use a word from the box to write the compound word shown by the picture.

| worm | driver | storm | ball | ache | flake | port | water |

1. foot _ball_

2. air_____

3. earth_____

4. rain_____

5. snow_____

6. screw_____

7. tooth_____

8. thunder_____

More to think about

1. Write the compound word shown by the pictures.

a)  = _buttercup_

b)  = _____

c)  = _____

d) = _____

2. Now write four more compound words.
   For each word, draw pictures of the two small words
   that make up the compound word.

Now try these

Copy these compound words. Split them into two small words.

1. pineapple = ___pine___ + ___apple___
2. seaweed = _____ + _____
3. upset   = _____ + _____
4. everyone = _____ + _____
5. funfair   = _____ + _____
6. aircraft = _____ + _____
7. afternoon = _____ + _____

Common expressions

Every day we use **common expressions** …

… of apology

… of greeting

… of surprise

… of warning

… of thanks

… of refusal

Practice

Copy these expressions. Say whether each is used for greeting someone or for saying goodbye.

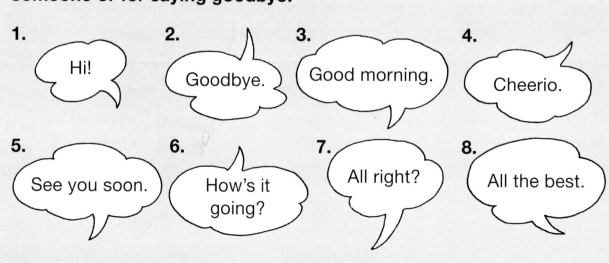

1. Hi!

2. Goodbye.

3. Good morning.

4. Cheerio.

5. See you soon.

6. How's it going?

7. All right?

8. All the best.

More to think about

Copy the table. Write each expression in the correct column.

Ways to express ...		
... apology	... warning	... thanks
Sorry.	Look out!	

Now try these

1. a) Write down as many common expressions of surprise as you can.

   b) Write down three occasions when you might use these expressions.

2. a) Write down as many common expressions of refusal as you can.

   b) Write down three occasions when you might use these expressions.

1. Use a dictionary to write a definition for each of these words.

   a)

   b)

   c)

   d)

   e)

2. Copy the sentences and choose the best dialogue word to complete them.

shouted	whispered	groaned	stuttered

   a) "I don't feel very well," the sick child _____.

   b) "Help! I've been robbed!" _____ the shopkeeper.

   c) "Don't wake up the baby," Mrs Samir _____.

   d) "It's a g… g… g… ghost," _____ the terrified boy.

3. Write what you think the underlined word in each sentence means.

   a) The passengers <u>abandoned</u> the sinking ship.

   b) The wicked <u>ogre</u> locked the princess in a tower.

   c) The paintbrush had no <u>bristles</u> left.

4. Copy these words and underline the root word in each of them.

    a) disappear   b) sadly   c) untie   d) trusting

5. Use a thesaurus to write a synonym for each of these words.

    a) wicked   b) ending   c) small   d) gloomy   e) walk

6. Write an antonym for each of these words.

    a) heavy   b) rough
    c) leave   d) catch
    e) empty   f) difficult
    g) walk   h) sharp
    i) huge   j) old

7. Copy the lists and match each word in Set A to its synonym in Set B.

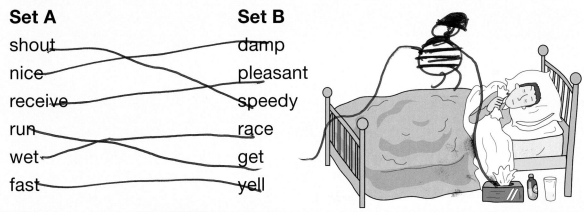

Set A	Set B
shout	damp
nice	pleasant
receive	speedy
run	race
wet	get
fast	yell

8. Write a homophone for each of these words.

    a) sow   b) sale
    c) won   d) flu

9. Write three words you might find in a dictionary between "shake" and "spear".

10. Write two compound words for each of these words.

a) snow

b) foot

c) fire

d) some

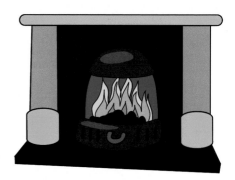

11. Copy the sentences.
Choose the most suitable homonym from the box to complete both sentences.

fair	wave	well	tie

a) Emma gave her mum a _____ from the boat.

   A big _____ splashed over the boat.

b) The referee said it was a _____ tackle.

   The _____ came to town.

c) I wear a _____ to school.

   I can _____ up my shoe laces.

d) I did not feel _____.

   You get water from a _____.

12. Write three common expressions for these everyday activities.

a) greeting someone   b) saying goodbye to someone